A Blind Girl's Survival

Copyright

Copyright 2020 Michelle Beary, The Author

Published in Winter Haven, FL. Published by Horton International Ministries, Inc.

All inquiries should be addressed to:

hortoninternationalministries@gmail.com

Print 1 – Volume 1 October, 2020

ISBN:

Foreword

by

Patricia Marcia Clarke

Michelle Beary is a dear, dear friend. If anyone could go through the struggles this lady has gone through and come out on top as she has…they are great and glorious people.

Our friendship began in Jamaica where we both lived and worked together at Jamaica Minister of Labor and Social Security. Michelle was a telephone operator who, although blind, would receive messages exactly as given and deliver exactly as given. Her work ethic was above many others as Michelle strived to always do her best.

I have known this lady for 25 years and during those years she has not always had things at her fingertips. She has not always been able to have everything she wanted, but, managed somehow through all her life struggles to get what she needed.

Michelle had many struggles in Jamaica as life was hard and I can attest to that. Life was hard for me even though I wasn't blind so imagine the trials and challenges for a person without vision.

Through all her struggles Michelle raised two children on her own. She was always pleasant to everyone, never raised her voice in anger, went out of her way to help others; and, as quickly as she learned about something, she shared it with those of us who didn't know.

Michelle's quest to learn more and do more often put her in the position as the "go to" person when anyone had a problem or question they could not solve. If she did not have an answer she would research and get back to you with some alternatives.

I cannot find the right words to describe this woman who has certainly lived "A Blind Girl's Survival", and lived it with determination. I can only wish the best to my dear, dear friend, and I'm sure you will enjoy reading her story as she takes you through the different chapters of her life.

Contents

Introduction

Life has been easy and life has been hard! It has been challenging and it has been fulfilling! So where do I start? I suppose I should start by telling you, yes, I am blind; but no, I was not born blind. As you read this story you will understand how and when my blindness occurred. The big thing is you will also learn how I survived!

Kingston is the largest city and the capital of Jamaica. Most people today know Kingston, Jamaica because of Bob Marley. The famous Bob Marley museum sits right in the middle of the City.

Kingston is the largest English speaking city south of the United States. It was not until the 1960's that major developmental changes started to occur in the center of Kingston.

Nearing the end of this decade was when I was born in Kingston, Jamaica and that will always be "home" to me. Kingston sits on the southeast corner of Jamaica and is known for the bustling downtown tourism and the ever present mountainous view.

These are the sights that entice the visitors. My family lived in Jamaica for many years and it was not until I was 38 years old that I was able to leave Jamaica.

There were challenges living in Jamaica. There were also good times and bad times. Some of these times I can recall as painful memories and others as miracles.

By the time I was two years old, my mother had another child; Sandra. Later on she had another girl; Carmen. My mother had a total of seven children; three boys and four girls. We do not all share the same fathers, but this is not unusual for the community where we lived.

Let me stop here before your thoughts run away! My mother was a decent, hard-working woman who had the same drudgeries of life casted upon her because of poverty, living conditions, human nature, and the societal system of Jamaica as everyone else.

I will capture the pain and the glory of my life but shed no ill feelings or blame on anyone else in my family or on Jamaica.

My Mother

Now you may think what mother would send her children away to live with someone else who has more children than her own? There is no need to wonder. I'll tell you. My mother was the sweetest person living. She was the product of a system of society that did not care much for Jamaicans, and even less for female Jamaicans.

My mother was abused by her "husbands" over the years. My stepfather hit my mother in her eyes. He would break the furniture. You see, my Mom was one of the females who believed she needed a man to help care for her and her children.

What I eventually learned about life, I have put together through my own life experiences and observations of the cultures of people around me. Without sight, I gained a keen sense of hearing and understanding.

My blindness was really hard for my Mom to accept. Until her death, when I was the person responsible for taking care of her, she believed that I was limited because of being blind. To the contrary, I have learned and accomplished so many things to help myself and others, as you can tell. Let's get back to my Mother.

My mother acted as if I was sighted like everyone else. I believe it was difficult for her as I never heard her say, "…this is my daughter who is blind." In fact, to her death, when I cared for her and my brother who was sick, I never heard my mom use the word "blind".

When she would shop for a dress for herself, she would ask me, "…doesn't this dress look good, what do you think about the color?" It was as if she wanted to believe that I visualized her in the dress as she could not or would not accept the fact that I was unable to see it.

If my Mom wanted to rearrange the furniture she would ask, "…do you think this chest looks better on this side or on the other side?" This may have been so I was aware of where the furniture is placed in the room. But it always came out as if she felt I could see the furniture.

It seemed my Mother was embarrassed about my blindness and attempted to shield me from other people in the community. I often wonder if my Mother did not talk about life and life situations because she had such difficulty handling her own life.

I cared for my mother until her death in November, 2001.

My First Years

The first three years of my life was spent right there in Kingston, Jamaica. At the time, there were six of us, my three older brothers and two other sisters. As one the youngest of the family, I can remember this being play time for me.

My friends were of different complexions and race. Although the majority of Jamaicans are of African descent, there are a number of other ethnic groups in Jamaica. These groups include Chinese, East Indians, Europeans and Syrians and Lebonese who are the most influential groups not only in Kingston but all of Jamaica. It is well known the darker skinned Jamaicans are generally at the lower sector of the socio-economic scale.

The ethnicity of my family is evident in our dark skin. This presented the normal challenges of housing, sufficient food supply, how to survive and live peacefully in the society.

Both my mother and father worked at menial jobs to support the family. This meant they were away from me and my siblings for long periods of time. The socio-economic class system did not protect families with children, and eventually my mother needed to make decisions about where best we might be able to live.

Apartment and homeowners were not freely willing to rent to some families with children. And as you know now, there were six of us – children. At the time, my parents were unable to find affordable housing that would accept children.

As difficult as the decision may have been for my mother, she made the best decision she felt at the time which was to take us to live with her sister.

My Aunt

Aunt Mary, my mother's sister, who took me and my siblings in when my mother was unable to find a place for us to live together, has a generous heart. I learned as I grew to an adult that there was but so much Aunt Mary could give us or do for us. In actuality, she gave everything she had which at the time was very little.

As I look back over my life and the way of life Aunt Mary and my mother lived, they were strong women who made do with what they had – no matter what.

These were women who without realizing it had skills and strength beyond measure to live in the conditions and under the pressures of the men of their time. Watching how Aunt Mary continued to live her life regardless of what she had or what she needed, gave me the strength and mind to know that I could be strong and survive as well.

I am truly grateful to Aunt Mary for the little things I learned about life from her, such as how to make lemonade from lemons rather than complain about the bitterness.

Moved

At the age of three, I was sent with my three other siblings to live with my maternal aunt who lived in the "country". The "country" is the rural area of Jamaica and Kingston is the urban or "town" area of Jamaica. Parallel the magnificence of Kingston, the City, with the country view of Bunkers Hill Clarendon, Jamaica. Bunkers Hill is approximately 92.8 km from Kingston, in the country.

Four of us were sent to live with this aunt. Two older brothers were already living in the country with a different aunt. We were sent to the country so that it would be easier for my mother and father to work and have a means of providing for all of us.

Imagine, a three year old without her mother and father is difficult enough. However, living with an aunt and uncle who had six children of their own, didn't make my life any easier.

I am convinced that my aunt wanted to do the best she could for my siblings and I. But, again, how much can you do in a two bedroom house where ten children are now sleeping in two beds, boys in one bed and girls in the other?

When it comes to the simple necessities of life, it was minimal. There was no running water in the house so we used the stream or "gully" as we called it, to retrieve water for all our daily activities.

Every morning and every evening the children would make several trips to carry buckets of water from the stream to fill the tubs and barrels at the house for various personal purposes.

The water from the gully was used for drinking, cooking, and bathing. Laundry was done at the gully on a weekly and on an as needed basis when we needed clean clothing.

There was no electricity in this home at the time so we had to utilize kerosene lamp. This made reading and studying a bit of a challenge.

Life in the Country

The culture of Jamaican living is that families will help each other whenever and wherever we can. My aunt and uncle took us in to help my mother, who at the time was experiencing extreme hardship in Kingston.

One thing I want you to understand, my mother did not desert us. Despite being the strong woman that she was, she made a decision that epitomizes her strength. This was to work hard and do whatever she needed to do to provide for her children while helping my aunt. This was not how my mother planned it; but this was the hand she was dealt and she was not going to abandon us.

My mother worked for pennies in Jamaica and sent money to my aunt to help with the household needs. In the country, we didn't have an extensive grocery bill or even gasoline for travel. We didn't even have a clothing bill. You may ask why? And the answer is because most of these things we supplied for ourselves and we were lacking in wealth so we couldn't purchase anything additional.

Although there were many of us in one house, there were happy times as well as trying times. In Jamaica, Christmas is the most festive time of the year; it is very similar to Thanksgiving in America. Christmas day was celebratory and joyous for my siblings and me. It's the day that families come together to eat, drink and be merry, but it was more special for us because my mother would come to the country to visit and spend the day with us. What a joy! I got to see my mother, be close to her, hug her, feel her presence and the love she had for us all.

Farming was a way of life in the country, and included raising pigs, goats, cows and chickens. The chickens produced eggs which were sold to neighbors or exchanged for other foods.

We grew our own food in vegetable gardens where ground produce such as yams, potatoes and bananas were plentiful.

As for clothing, we had one pair of shoes for special occasions like church. I remember having many cuts on my feet from walking barefooted. "Hand me downs" were also very common in the country. Clothes were passed down from one child to the next with rarely a new piece of clothing appearing.

Despite the happy times at Christmas, I felt the country experience was terrible. Being away from my mother was the greatest challenge. My aunt did the best she could to provide for us but she showed favoritism towards her children. At times I felt like running away or hurting myself. Overall, the experience of living with this aunt was abusive—physically, mentally and emotionally and yes, I even considered killing myself at times.

Let me give an example. My cousins, my aunt's children, could do no wrong in her sight. So my siblings and I received the discipline for things my cousins often did. My aunt would hide the money my mom sent to provide for us. We did not receive or get to enjoy any of my mother's hard-earned money and my aunt would curse after she removed and hid the money from the envelope.

I appreciate my aunt for taking us in her home. But would you believe she fed her children and send my siblings and me to bed with only a cup of tea or sometimes a cup of water? Often times we had just two meals; breakfast and dinner, and at school, we had no lunch. Sometimes my siblings and I brought ground provisions (yams, bananas from the garden) as our lunch or to exchange with someone else for food at lunchtime.

My aunt had two dogs. One was called Blackman and the other was called Shadow. Whenever we misbehaved, my aunt would tell

Blackman to chase us, and indeed, he listened to her. Blackman would catch and pin us down for my aunt to discipline us. She mostly did this to my siblings and I because, remember, her children could do nothing wrong.

When I say the country, I want to paint the right picture. There were no hospitals, shopping malls, grocery stores, city hall, museums or salons. We were just ordinary people living as best we knew how to survive.

Each of my aunt's children was born inside her house. When she went into labor the other children were dispersed to neighbors until after the delivery. When we returned there would be a new baby and chores would be reassigned so that my aunt could attend the baby.

As for doctors, there were none in the country. Serious illnesses that were not relieved or cured by remedies handed down through generations required going into Kingston.

Here in rural Jamaica if we needed to reach someone outside of our area, we wrote notes, called urgent messages and took them to the Post Office for delivery. In most cases, it was easier and sometimes faster, to give the note to someone going to town to bring for delivery. Then again, sometimes it was just simpler and easier to send a message without writing a note.

Christmas wasn't the only joyous time. As children we played cricket, baseball, ring games and other games we probably made up. My aunt would sometimes play with us. She would also walk with the ten of us to local concerts and gatherings. We walked everywhere as we had no car.

Sunday School was the weekly highlight. We all learned verses from the Bible that we needed to recite before eating Sunday dinner.

I have always been afraid of rats and frogs. As punishment, my aunt would catch a rat to throw on me. I disliked going to the gulley to get water because of my fear of frogs.

The five years I spent in the country were a part of my survival. These are the years through which my strong survival all began. Life is such, that when you look back, you are able to learn from the things you have been through.

The Shift

The years I spent in the country are memorably difficult as well as pleasantly surprising. Those years taught me the agony of being worse than poor.

As a child, I did not know what "abuse" might be. It is only after going through each of these phases that I can now identify the mental, physical, emotional and sexual abuse I have experienced. Where and when did my life shift?

While still living in the country, I had the greatest impact in my life. Depending on how you look it at, it may be my curse or my blessing. As my older sister and I were playing on our way to school one morning, we were teasing and joking with each other as we often did. My sister said her friend was going to give her a gift. Of course, I didn't believe her and said she was lying. At this my sister threw a small rock towards me which unintentionally hit me in the left eye.

Unfortunately, there was no immediate medical attention but my aunt provided the best homemade care she could until the following day. She brought me to Kingston because there were no children's hospital in the country and my aunt saw that I needed immediate medical attention. Despite the healing properties in the "leaves or bush", she saw that my eye needed greater medical care. This was my first visit to a medical clinic, at the age of eight.

I lost temporary vision in both eyes immediately after the incident. After five weeks in The Children's Hospital in Kingston, I regained sight temporarily in the right eye.

In the 1990's after experiencing vision issues for approximately 20 years, I permanently lost sight in both eyes after developing an infection due to the lack of proper care.

Naturally, my sister was hurt about this tragedy and at the same time my sense was that she did not want to be with me, now that I had a deformity. The accident and resulting blindness lead to my return to Kingston to live with my mom again, so at least one good thing came out of it.

I was the second of my siblings to return to Kingston and slowly but surely, we all moved back to Town to live with my mom.

My Father

I knew very little about my biological father. Later in life I learned that when he heard that I was returning to Kingston, as a child, he left my mother. When I returned to Kingston from the country my mother was living with my stepfather.

Although I had no contact with my father over the years, at age 27 I decided to look for him. Before leaving Kingston for New York I was able to find him and organized a trip to visit him.

We had an enjoyable visit. Nothing would ever replace the years we lost, however, in my spirit I felt at peace that I found my father and was able to let him know I loved him.

My father died while I was in New York and I paid for my sister to attend his funeral as I was not able to attend. May he rest in peace with whatever memories he has!

Return to Kingston

It was a difficult adjustment living as a blind person. I didn't attend school for six years. My Mom and family, as well as myself, had to come to an acceptance of the blindness. Honestly, I believe I was able to accept blindness for what it is and move on to do what is needed to live. I am not sure that my mom ever fully accepted my blindness.

Now, remember, I was still a child. I was only eight years old when I returned to Kingston. My father was no longer in the picture and my stepfather; who is the father of my youngest sister came to live with us in the family home.

I'm assuming because I was blind, my stepfather felt he would be able to sexually assault me without any recompense, no problem…she's blind what can she say? This is what was probably going through his mind.

Well, it wasn't what I said it was what I did. I resisted his fondling, and as a result was verbally and physically abused by both my Mom and stepfather. My Mom was reluctant to do anything about this abuse.

She felt she should protect me from being abused by anyone by keeping me at home, while neglecting the fact that there was a main predator in the home. She was terribly afraid of what would happen to me, a young blind girl in Kingston.

My stepfather's attempt of sexual abuse was the first, but not the last. At age 11, a Jamaican soldier in Kingston attempted rape me. I told my mother what happened and she blamed me, screamed and cursed at me as if I was the guilty one.

My mother felt these sexual advances were somehow initiated by me while I innocently was the victim. It was difficult to talk with my mother about sex, life, a woman's role or what my feelings should be. I wasn't able to discuss these situations with her. Everything was blamed on me. It seemed to me everything I did was wrong.

How many times have you heard, "if I knew then what I know now?" Well, I knew nothing, I repeat nothing, about life, puberty, sex, menstruation, child birth, delivery; how children are conceived or born. This was a subject my mother never brought up but in her own way felt she was protecting me because of my blindness.

I remember vividly, I was cleaning the house one day, at the age of 12, when my mother noticed my clothes were soiled and she yelled and cursed at me to take a shower and change clothes. Guess what???? I started menstruating, my period started. She did not explain what was happening but told me to use toilet paper or cloth to avoid staining my clothes. It wasn't until age 16 that I learned to use sanitary napkins.

After the attempt of abuse at age 11, I was locked in the house for three months because my mom was embarrassed and I was embarrassed. How could a defenseless blind young girl defend herself against such attacks?

My Mom did domestic work and I went with her to tend the children outside while she worked. One day when we returned to our rented home and prepared for bed we began to experience serious itching and insufferable pain. That's when we realized that the landlady had placed cowitch leaf in the beds to evict us from the home. Cowitch leaf is a type of plant that, when it comes in contact with the skin, it causes uncontrollable itching.

My stepfather was verbally and physically abusive towards my mother. On May 11, 1981 Bob Markley died. I remember his death as that was also the day my stepfather left us all. Now my mom had to make it on her own.

Those were the days that I remember the conviction I had to become the strong woman I am today. With most of my family not believing in the abilities I have, and, survival being important for everyone, I decided I would learn everything I could. I would apply the skills God gave me to not only help myself but to help others.

Not very long after, my mother got another job at a college and she was no longer able to take us to work with her. This is the beginning of my self-help, self-taught existence as I learned through caring for myself and being in the house continually again. I learned how to clean, cook, do domestic chores and be responsible for my siblings, even the older ones.

School

About this time, a member of the community reported to the authorities that I was not attending school. The fact that the truancy had been reported didn't change my mother's idea about me not going to school. Instead, we moved to another area to avoid my enrollment in school.

Eventually, we learned about The Salvation Army School for the Blind in Kingston, where I was enrolled at age 14 into the 3rd grade. This was the only school in Jamaica with the capabilities to tend to blind or visually impaired children.

There are times now that I feel I suffered for those years when I lost a formal education. At the Salvation Army School for the Blind, I quickly learned braille, life skills and how to further handle and care for myself in various situations.

Not only did I learn academics but as a boarding student, who went home on the weekends, I learned the most valuable lessons of life and how to interact with other people, both sighted and non-sighted.

Rojeanna, the sister who is two years my senior and the one who caused the accident, was responsible for picking me up from school. By this time, cruelty showed itself as Rojeanna was embarrassed and would hide my face so that people would not look at my eyes as we passed. At times, she walked before me as if we were not together.

Because I couldn't see, Rojeanna would take my things and hide them because she felt she should have everything better than me. Now, she looks to me for guidance. Fortunately we no longer have those silly fights that we used to have as kids.

I graduated in 1987 from The Salvation Army School for The Blind at age 18. This is quite an accomplishment in itself as this was the strength of my conviction to help myself in every way possible. I finished high school and went on to additional training with great determination.

My Daughter

I was age19 when she was born, just after I graduated from The Salvation Army School for the Blind. As you will see, I had many mishaps and conceiving my daughter before marriage was one of those things that happened but I have no regrets for having her.

Now, I do not blame anyone. I'm not pointing fingers, but, I can say truthfully that being blind actually left me open to some abuses that a sighted person may not have faced. Jerlene's father did not live with us or marry me.

My daughter excels in whatever she does. She has grown to be an educated adult who has a profession that she loves. We lived together in New York and this daughter worked, went to school, attended to my needs and ran a household.

The strength and courage my daughter has come directly from me. She has seen some of the abuses that I've suffered and she has also seen how I came through each of them. This, I believe, makes my daughter, Jerlene, the woman she is today.

At two years old my daughter began to learn the denominations of money. So, she was naturally my financial adviser, my banker, my money bag. Jerlene would tell me what money I had, count it, provide and verify change correctly. She is a financial wizard.

It is no wonder that as she prepared to attend college and we didn't have the money for registration, a complete stranger stepped up and gave her the money needed.

Jerlene assumed the role of father for her brother. She is his father and second mom. She provides moral and financial support.

Like myself, Jerlene will be a perennial learner. She has a Bachelor of Science degree in Psychology, and an Associate Degree in Criminal Justice. She is now married and is going to college for Nursing.

This daughter is my mobility teacher. She is patient with me and guides me through technology so that I can continue to learn.

My daughter is Mommy's blessing!

My Adult Journey

After graduation in 1987, and while living with my mother, I started school in the evenings for telephone operating while working at a local furniture manufacturer. The feel/touch, smell and hearing senses become keener as these senses are relied upon heavily by someone who has no sight.

I developed a tremendous sense of feel and worked in the sanding department of the furniture manufacturer. It was my responsibility to assure each piece was smooth, without flaw, bumps or blemishes.

For three years I worked at this job and cannot recall any pieces that I handled being rejected or sent back as imperfect. We made wooden souvenirs and kitchen items which were shipped to Europe and throughout the world.

This phase of my life also started my Christian journey. I became more independent, travelling to and from work on my own while caring for my daughter.

I started attending Bible study at a Seventh Day Church of God. I also attended parties, movies, met with friends and felt comfortable moving around Kingston on my own.

Then, one night after Bible Study, I was robbed by three men who held me at knife point. I suffered a nervous breakdown following this incident. This is mostly as a result of my distrust of the local authorities. They would not believe anything that is reported to them by a blind person. The police in Jamaica dismiss concerns of blind people as if we have no sense. So the incident was never reported.

I experienced fear, desperation, humiliation, unraveling of my self-confidence, and became doubtful that now I could be hopeful not helpless. It was generally the viewpoint of the authorities that how do I know I was robbed, how would I know who robbed me? After all I could not see them.

There are other blind people that I know who were physically and sexually abused. They have not been able to report these abuses or tell anyone about what happened to them. My strength comes from my Mom and her sister, my aunt. I thank God for them. I learned from them to face the challenges of this world and do what I needed to do to keep going.

My Son

Although blind since 1977, I have lived a full life. There are many blind people who do not get the opportunity to experience love from others, to be married, to grow strongly in faith or to have children who they can nurture.

I am blessed to experience unconditional love from my two children. After 10 fulfilling years with my daughter, God blessed me with my handsome son. My son is a special person. (Note: I believe all mothers feel this way, but, I am serious when I say, my son is a special person). My son has become a strong man in his household and throughout the struggles of being raised by a blind mother he has grown to be like my husband.

My son, Erroll, is the person who knows all my medications. Erroll knows when my doctor appointments are and who my doctors are. He takes care of my needs and keeps me in the know of what's happening in the neighborhood.

This is the person who takes me wherever I need to go and waits patiently until I am finished and ready to leave. My son was born in Jamaica but has spent most of his life in the United States.

Having children wasn't as difficult as raising them without visibility. You know, God's hand is always with you. As I feel the creases of my son's forehead and the shape of his nose, the curve of his mouth from a baby I can tell you when he approaches without saying a word.

There are certain senses that become more prominent to a blind person. I can sense the smell of my son, with or without cologne. I can tell his voice from near or far, on the phone or in person. This handsome young man is the rock of my life and always will be. God has blessed me to raise him to be the man that he has become.

When my son was born, I was praying for another girl. But when he was laid in the bed bedside me I knew he was sent to me for a special reason. It's a miracle that he is with me.

My son will always be a special gift in my life!

My House

My confidence was shaken for awhile, however, after the training as a telephone operator I worked for the Jamaican government as a switchboard operator for 14-1/2 years.

During this part of my life I obtained my own home where my daughter, my son and I lived. My home was open to many who lived with us when they had no place to go.

My house wasn't a big one; it was just a studio sized home where some times as many as ten people lived. I made life easier for those who were temporarily homeless. Although I can't see, it gives me great joy to hear the smile in someone's voice when I am able to help them.

Life with my son's father made me realize that I was a victim of domestic violence—just like my Mom. My son's father lived with us for a few years. To get away, the two children and I would visit friends and relatives in the United States for Christmas.

When I lived with this man, the physical abuse grew stronger and more violent. He threatened our lives on more than one occasion. When my son was three years old, his father hit me and threatened to kill us with a machete. My daughter was not able to stop him from beating me, but my son stepped in and pounded with his fists. This stopped his rage.

After so much physical abuse I got a restraining order to put him out of my home and out of my life. Life for the three of us was hard but easy because we had each other.

New York

At this point, I am a blind working, single parent that has learned how to care for herself and her children. I was determined to not live a life of physical, mental or emotional abuse—after all I was blessed to be alive and blessed to live for others, especially my children.

The children and I began to travel to New York to visit friends at least once a year. We went several times in the summer but mostly around Christmas. This is where I met a wonderful, loving and caring man who would become my husband and a father to my children.

In 2007 we moved to New York from Jamaica and lived happily for some time. New York, New York that wonderful town is where I really found myself.

I consider myself a helpful and caring person. This led to the development of many friendships. When I was working in Jamaica I helped the elderly with their pensions, was able to give to those who needed help (although I probably needed help myself and didn't realize it). These same people assisted me and my kids on the journey of our migration to America.

The journey I've made has helped me to realize that if you can help someone each day with a word, a song, any small thing then your living will not be in vain.

The City of New York is so much easier to navigate with subways, buses, sidewalks and paved roads. This made it simpler for me to learn to get around the city. I developed hobbies and became skilled at touring the streets of New York on my own.

My community was close knit and we knew our neighbors. Everyone looked after each other similar to the families in Jamaica. A part of my contribution to this community was babysitting for mothers who needed help, and saving two people from committing suicide with my words of encouragement.

I did babysitting and hair braiding for those in the community, often times, without pay. However, I feel because of my disability I amazed my friends with what I was able to do for myself. Often people would ask if I was fooling the public, and could really see.

My love and caring for others allowed me to teach young families how to live and manage their households. Eventually, I went to work at Goodwill Industries in New York doing book scanning. This is where I learned computer skills.

As I mentioned, the streets of New York were easier to navigate so I was able to go by myself to places that would not have been accessible to a blind person in Jamaica.

I worked at Goodwill Industries, where as usual, it had always been important to me to do my best at each job and to learn something new. I am always learning so I am always progressing.

Michelle Beary

If given the chance, blind people would prove to the world the things we can do for ourselves. Blindness doesn't hold me back. People hold me back. I still have dreams of travelling and telling God's goodness.

When it comes to problems, the way out is to trust God on the way through. Being a Christian and living righteously as God intended is what helps me each day to get through the day. There have been times when I could "see" no way, but thank God for provided a way.

Married

What drew me to New York and what kept me in New York was the husband I met during those visits to my friends.

Married life and the joy of freedom to move about in the community was a pleasurable experience for me. It is obvious to you by now that I am always trying to help others and find joy in my life by doing things for other people.

My husband at the time expected that I should be solely dependent upon him. I suppose because of being blind he felt I should not have independence but be the homemaker who cooked, cleaned, did laundry fed him and the children and just sit in the house and be happy.

The newly found ability to use public transportation to go wherever I pleased, shop, dance, enjoy music and movies, empowered me to be independent and still be a good wife and mother.

Soon, my husband and I were divorced. However, this ex-husband and I have a friendly relationship as he now calls on me to handle his finances and legal business.

My kids and I lived with a friend in New Jersey for a while after my divorce to get back on my feet again. This living arrangement was broken when we returned back to the house one day to find the gate to the house locked and we could not enter.

Although this was a terrifying life event, at the moment I felt content because bearing tragic and unexpected events in life have become "bumps in the road" for me. We, of course, found other living arrangements and got through that tragedy.

It is with this thought I close… I am forever thankful and praise God for the wonders He does for me. I am thankful that God has allowed me to experience this life and it is my hope to share my journey with others. Why? Just to let you know that there is always a way, just trust God.

Despite the challenges in life, I am pleased with what I have accomplished. I believe life can be a fulfilling experience as having a disability does not limit you. With God, self-motivation and determination, you can achieve all your dreams and aspirations. I thank God, my mother, my aunt, my siblings; and, most of all for my children being a part of my life and creating an impact in this *"Blind Girl's Survival."*

From the Publisher

I have the privilege of publishing many stories, some of joy, some of sadness, some of heartaches, some of power, some with spiritual uplifting. Never have I had the opportunity to work with such a wonderful person as Michelle Beary, Author.

We have not physically met. We have only met for a virtual meeting where I was able to "see" the author. She has not seen me, however, the days and times we spent together capturing the realism of her pain, struggles and how she has become such a strong woman makes me feel as if I have known her all my life.

I believe that the author has "seen" me in her spirit and I love her and wish her the best with telling the world her story about survival.

Blessings and Joy, Michelle.

Faye Saxon Horton

A Blind Girl's Survival

Available to order directly from Michelle Beary @ kattiecamp@gmail.com

Available from Amazon.com.

Ebook

Print Book

Audio Book